A Cat's Day

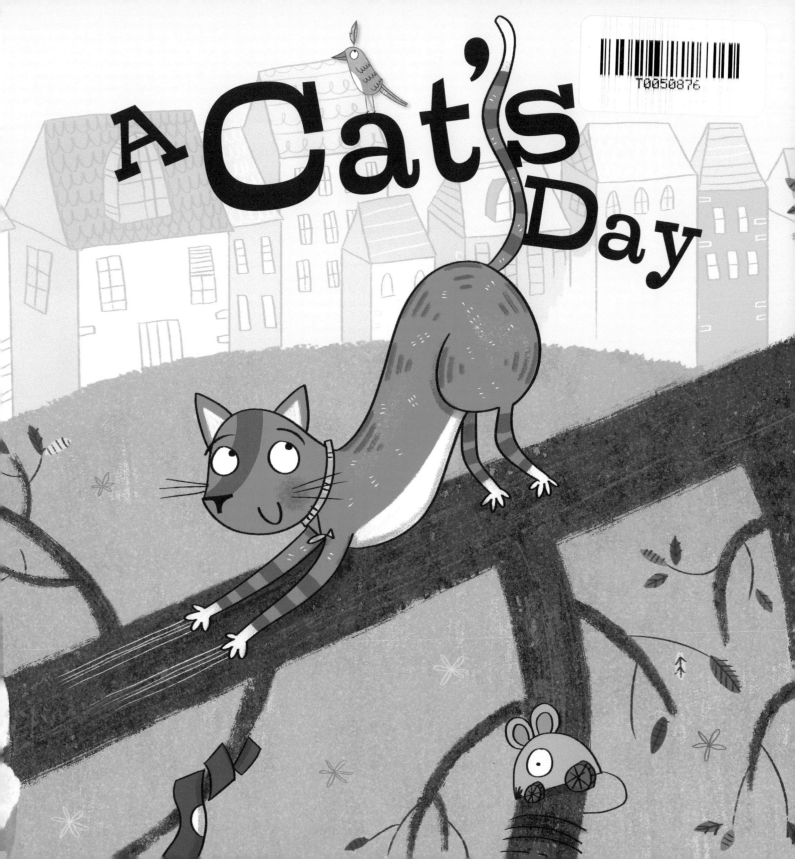

"What a beautiful morning," Lucy the cat thought.

"I think I'll have an adventure today!"

As soon as Lucy was sure Boy
had left for school, she leapt out
of the window.

"Silly Boy," Lucy thought. "He never notices when I leave!"

Lucy's first stop was her favorite tree.
It was always full of squirrels to chase.

"These squirrels can really move!" Lucy thought to herself as she leapt after a squirrel with a bushy tail.

Soon Lucy decided it was time for a snack. "I'm getting hungry!" she thought.

Luckily, she wasn't far from the supermarket. Lucy crept inside and tore open a bag of cat food.

"Yum! This is delicious!" she purred.

Then Lucy spotted an angry-looking supermarket worker, "Uh oh," Lucy thought. "Better get out of here!

Lucy visited the pet shop next. It was
always full of toys, treats, and fish!

Lucy chased a toy mouse. "Don't mind me, little mouse," she meowed.

Next, Lucy slipped into the clothing store. She leapt into a basket of soft socks.

"This sock will be
a great new toy!"
she thought.

Then Lucy heard a familiar
voice. It was Boy!

"I should get home!"
Lucy thought.

Lucy got home just in time!
Boy was just walking in the door.

When Luke got home, he put down his bags.

He had a lot of homework to do tonight. He was going to write about tigers.

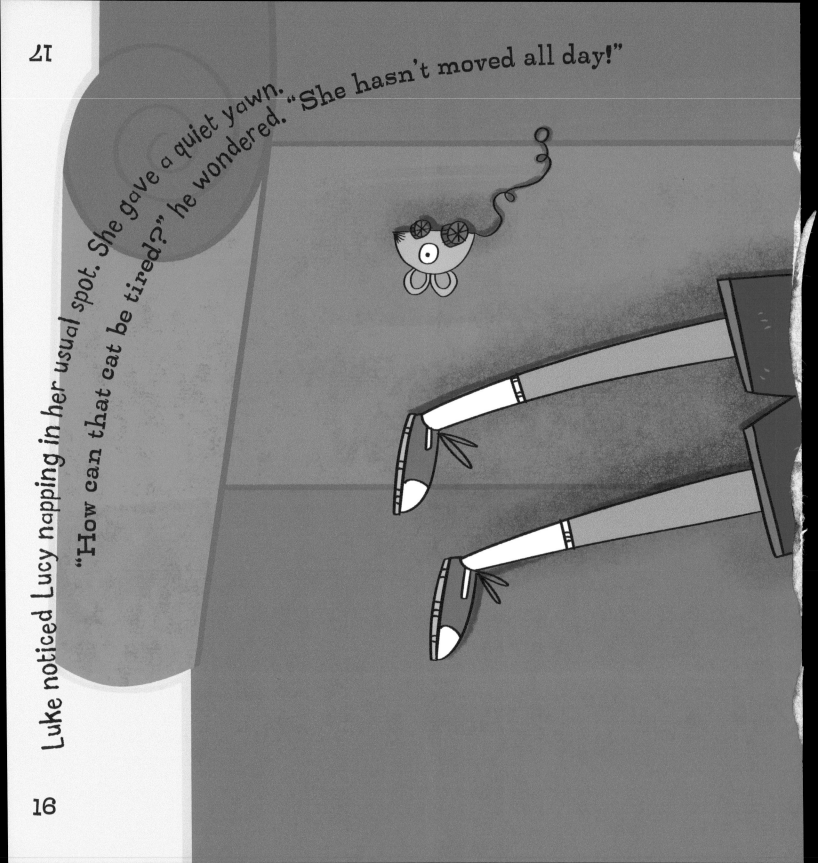

Luke noticed Lucy napping in her usual spot. She gave a quiet yawn.

"How can that cat be tired?" he wondered. "She hasn't moved all day!"